An Afternoon With God

Amble V Riaanardh

An Afternoon With God - A Collection of Poems

Published by Riaanardh Publishers

Sandton, South Africa

ollive1000@gmail.com

ISBN 978-0-620-94517-2

eISBN 978-0-620-94518-9

2 4 6 8 10 9 7 5 3 1

Layout and cover design by Boutique Books

Printed in South Africa

This collection of poems is dedicated to:

my parents, Paddy and Sarie Padayachee

and

my English teacher, Mr. R. Singh

Contents

I LIVE POETRY

"I hate poetry!" they silently swore,
"POETS LIKE CRIMINALS DON'T FOLLOW THE LAW!"
"We rack our properly educated brain,
… for something blurred, absurd and so insane…
WHAT'S WRONG WITH THIS CURT, FORMIDABLE LOT,
DRIVE US MAD; THAT'S THEIR INSIDIOUS, PLAIN PLOT!"

… Now let's look at your grievance
You might decide on lenience…

Each faceted word, chiseled
Each comma, emotion-filled!

This language of God spoken, not plainly, but true
Seeps like breath into life, deep within,
Inside you
These words, born, suckled, bred; not for eye and ear...
It's life force – only the soft heart can bear

So next, if you endeavor,
God's chosen words, SAVOUR!

God's words process through heart
then soul,
Fall to the past; see how it's told!

A kneading of love and truth, intricate
Thoughts, words, deeds, demonic and delicate.
With that constant, sacred golden, coiled Thread
God's lessons and love, unsparingly spread!
If ever you've fallen in love deep and true,
Yes, God's language you spoke, unbeknownst to you…

AN AFTERNOON WITH GOD

A gentlest breeze
A careless caress
All emotions cease
All this space more or less …

The soothing shade
The singing grass
A wooden swing; man-made
A multi-colored bird flies pass!

A teasing river
The lurking black rocks
makes my soul quiver
As shepherds pass, guiding flocks.

I sip my tea with a pensive sigh
Then I talk seriously with God –
I dare to look straight in the Eye,
"I don't mean to be unholy, my sweet LORD,

-The miracle workings of a fly?
-The life-giving umbilical cord!
-A universe in a cell…. do Defy
Our elusive minds, DEAR GOD!

There are some of us out here,
cuffed hands… eyes searching the sky.
Craving scathing penance to bear…
For you, God … Prepared to die!

Are our hearts tainted so…?
Have we fallen so far, so deep, so low?
So screaming souls suffocate in silence?
Allow us please, some penitence!"

"Many a pearl rolled to sin"
THEN… A deep breath sucked; whirling me in!
The universe, minute at my feet…
Billions of years in this moment fleet…

Altered time in a myriad mystical heavens
Spirits of me, luminous in spiritual taverns!
Past ones in whiteness, lightness, brightness
And truly angelic ones… NOW BLESS!

Rows and rows of blackened Pearls
Slip, sizzling into a soul dip!
After a million miles of smokey curls
Shaded grey spirits pop out for the homeward trip!

In a lightning flash I clasp my cup!
"Did I ANSWER…? DID YOU SEE…?"
Shaken and shocked … l barely look up…
" YOU, THE UNIVERSE, IS ABSOLUTELY ME!"

Craving, agitated … I pour more tea,
This herbal, potentially potent potion…
Invokes a trance in me,
I look within, stirring a nostalgic notion!

Swirling, humming … now I see,
Shackles of shame; mired mind in motion!
If I tried; saintly could I be?
No instant balm, no soothing lotion

A concoction of egoism, lust, lies,
greed, anger, hatred, deceit…..
Blackened my spirit under a guise…
Shedding!…. This lifetime's only feat!

I drink my very last drop!
Soaring love envelopes me tight
An eternally spreading field of golden crop
My naked soul, a blinding white light!

Now the night sky it's opulence beams
Cradling darkness, dazzling my tiny world!
I look at this world, so far it seems
Swirling lightness, I'm curious and curled!

I FELL IN LOVE WITH DEATH

Fell in love with Death,

kissed, helled and caressed

In his safe, strong coffin in peace I rest …

Is death even reality, if I die piecefully everyday

awakening I take a deep breath, of mustiness

unmoving numb dangling in tangles anyway

Death, pensively stalks my heart's laughter

Daily, my fortune he greedily saps of merit

Death strangled success that I was after…

Still, eyes my soul's flickering, fiery spirit!

He gripped my diseased, malaised heart.

Death ripped my soul and tore it apart

Ransacked my tortured, derailed mind.

In Death's love yet only shelter I find

prepared to die for the love of Death

Bathe in a milky ocean of rebirth,

Cocoon myself in carefree love,

Awaiting my, blazing, white dove.

THE SEA

Blessed was the morning,
Her expanse heaving and sighing,
That I looked out to sea…
And then, it occurred to me!

Sea is all woman,
… rock is but man
So soft, deep, fiery, meditative
So hard, strong, muscled, authoritative …

Dancing, ebbing teasingly around him
At her subservient whim,
His stature glistening in ruthless foreboding
As she softly enveloped, craving, deciding …

The mystic sea, a constant changing mood
And in her womb pulsated life-attesting food -
Reflected a varying color…
Perfected sustenance; strained to pallor!

Then, with the precisely cycled moon
…the tsunami came as a jilted boon…
Turning this nurturer into a violent predator!
Crushing in spitting the rock to glittering litter!

MY DEAREST SISTER SYLVIA

Dearest, Dearest, Sylvia
Of hearts so pure and parallel
The whole world will jeer,... sneer
This swollen heart's quell; yet I must tell …

I've wallowed in your glorious grave
Your ashes I still swallow!
Your soul; your soul; Help me to save!
Lord! I hear a buffalo bellow!

Save me; Save me, I am insane!
Lunar monsters; to the death they fight…
How excruciating was your pain?
Look at my hand!... I took a savage, lethal bite!

Help me save your soul
I've forsaken myself; he hates me!
Only you can scrape me together, whole!
You light up; I'll redeem us, you'll see.

Do you really love me so?
You reached into this demonic sea,
You had watched me sink so low,
But when we touched, it was for ETERNITY!

That shuddering touch
Torched spirit, singed mind; Slit heart
One Of A Kind …. Karma is such …
Now chuck the space that keeps us apart!

In my heart; a faint beat doubled
Now this lilting light from the past
soothes this soul so troubled …
Hold me Sylvia; Please let it last!

My beloved, I see you so clearly
You rise in the bursting, benevolent sun,
Moan with the moon, you plea
Hand in hand, breathlessly we run …

You hold my hand, I breathe
Cells swirl in a transcendental twirl
Now life and love freed
Oh! smooth, soothing, satisfying pearl..

Cupped in my hand; to my heart
I treasure; I resuscitate
of which we are a part
I nurture this soul's only mate.

SUICIDE NOTE TO MY SWEETHEART

I did my best,
I'm setting you free.
If I betrayed you, then, I betrayed me!

My essence was lost
when, to your way I was forced.
This time my love be softer, gentler
Protect and nurture the magic find, that's her!
Usher her lovingly into your world…
Let her dreams come true when you see her Curled.

Respect and appreciate her, the world will too!
Offerings reverently at your feet, that she'll do!
Fight the world ; not a love so true!
She'll not fail you, the way you say I do…
Simply my love, keep her strong and secure
Prevention is better, wait there is no
cure!

If she weakens and you hear her call…
Forget money, heed, don't let her take that fall
Yes, money has muscle and glorious might…
My dear, it has no heart; you'll irk this plight
Please don't undermine her power…
Surely, when unleashed, you'll
cower!

If you must murder her will to grow,
Then do it mercifully because it will show!
If she resigns to cozy your home
Acknowledge, respect, cherish this poem
She'll do it all; even take the fall!
Be truthful when you say you didn't hear her call!

Love truly, so she'll not throw in the towel!

I DECIDE

As I approach the dusky woods
A walk, I decide, ...
I contemplate the shoulds
As life passes beside

Dry fallen twigs loudly snap
Tiny birds dart in fright!
Emotions too…once a trap,
Disappear into false, night!

The inmates of my prisoned, squalid mind
Stand shadowy, torturously, lurking in the dark
My past in every step I hear, loudly unkind
Distant, distinct light I see, growing ever stark

An intrigue cascades unsummoned
Wild thoughts defined… now refined
Heart unjaded
unlocks a beautiful mind!

And then I stepped willfully
To the blinding bright otherside …
"DID YOU DECIDE?" I heard distantly!
"NO…?" DID YOU SIMPLY ABIDE??"

MY SOUL IS A FOOL

My soul flies free with birds

It caresses the herds

My soul soars with eagles

Taking refuge in pills

My soul mingles with the blazing stars

It finds exhilaration in fast cars

My soul dives over a waterfall

And quietly listens to the evening call

My soul frolics in fire

Incinerates with desire

My soul revels openly

Chides and defies the lock and key

My soul dances in heaven

And crushed with 911

My soul drinks of pure passion

Even if it were poison

My soul is a foolish fling

And it has no brain, poor thing..!

Solely defied, defiled and cracked

Now lays open to redemption or attack!

JUNKYARD

There it screamed of hellish pain
And screeched at me viciously
This carnage, so brutally insane …

Once a marvel of prowess and prestige,
Power, pride, joy, comfort, love
Now a barrage of metal under siege

That intoxicating new-car smell
Heavenly pace, race of hearts,
A demise, making my taut throat quietly quell

"… she moves so well … what a beauty!"
He says, callously content.
Time ushers in reckless cruelty!

Wronged, Wrecked, Wretched, Wrangled, Metal
A sombre graveyard of crowded emptiness
Your core waits for anything. Will the dust Settle?

Then from the dust rises a soaring Messiah!
Recycling death, life-pumping tools.
Hope, Trust, Faith, Respect glisten from the pyre.

Is such utter dissolution accidental?
From such souls-shattering shambles
Arise smooth, shimmering subjects of true Metal!

THE CANDLE

I

have

only now

sincerely

seen

in

....

this   sacred   life's   fire,   unassuming

Cupped   palm,   I   hold   a   drop   of   sun

so   then I close   my eyes resuming.

My life; gently I breathe into her!!

Elementally   I   am   touched,   torched.

Caught in flames I kick, punch, stop

Calm I centre, see am not scorched!

Dancing in a flame, dicing in delight

Sinned religiosity spiraling declension

relinquish, white warmth, love, a light

silence slips, dissipating, an ascension

Sheds silently, still, straight, stay centre

This flame, a pith inside my every cell

God's benignly burning love's mentor

So serenely in the soul of souls, I dwell

then, a gentle breeze caresses my heat

Awakened; I stray.., I sway wild and falter

quivering so profusely, in virtuousness defeat

My dearest Lord, if only I stayed the flame at Thine Altar

QUIET MOMENTS

My bedroom, soft with salt crystal light

sacred, serene burrow
When atlast, I close the door to sorrow

I languish in perfumed, pink, pure, delight …
The sounds of the world dimmed

I cry, I sigh and am free at last
To fervently forget the tinged past

Swirls, curls; the future is brimmed …
This soft, snuggled moment a rarity

The slumberous universe I feel…
A whisper answering my soft appeal

The spun golden thread, my clarity!
Quietly I hear, listening in earnest

a pulsating, soft, deafening darkness
within a strong, tokened tenderness…

A universe within, so honest!
The comforting unknown studded space

penetrates, umbilically ignites; torches
chambers of my heart it nurtures

Mind, Soul, Intellect race!

HAVE YOU EVER KISSED A ROSE?

The reddest of a bloody red
pungent sweet scent of desire …
from a pure heart; blasé head
Passionate eyes permeating fire

To one fallen in mire
Hungrily she drew in
This gift of love's breath….
Tenderly she kissed sin
Relishing, laughing in mirth
This token from her lover
It's velvety lips openly flirt
A heart's honored preying guest
Caressed, poignantly appealing…
It slipped down
her neck
In a heart wrenching choke!
A passionate, lusty grip tightening
Whithering and resurging
Desuetude love divine
A precarious precious life-line …
Haloed arms widening!
This filthy, frustrating body….
A horrible transient thing!
OH! but for a sacrificial rose
I died… released,
This mundane love, a festering fling!

Then, His blood-drenched rose
Scented of heaven …..
Carved from His Heart
True Love He did impart
… stark to the masquerading mundane
Hungrily she drew in
This delicately folded gift from God…
Fixated, this nectar she kissed
Thinly sliced red heart; clenched fist
Now He was her Lord…!
It's velvety lips
Dazzling, dewed, dawning
Cascaded her crown
… her neck down
And her heart, it did, save!
Each day it infused, instilled still more…
Compassionate Love, Calm, Clarity

Through this sacred, precious life - string
she perceived love liberating.
Bathed in blood, Lord's magnanimity
The praying clasp of the bud
Flamboyance of love's fragility
Resigned, wuthering liberation
Final exoneration
The kiss… spiritual.

EVER FOLLOWED A WAVE?

A meticulously maternal horizon
Gives birth to a care-free wave
Dancing almost aimlessly with it's next of kin.
This far-off watery burp, so naive.

Dipping to dismay but always surfacing
with trifling trepidations; focussed direction
Only a keen eye breathlessly anticipating
Awaiting shorely; yes, it's resurrection

As this wonderous energy from churning came
gallantly, menacingly, striving forward
Ominously slipping playing life's cunning game
Ferociously clawing and frothing skywards

A symphony from heaven or even hell.
Eagerly eyes the shoreline with wealth
Effusive energy - none can quell
Forgivingly this time, into the sand it'll melt.

But like all intimacies of love and hate
That of a sea so deep and vast open land
Etched on the rock of fate
As waves of life turn hearts to sand....

A DULL DAY

A soft, drizzled caressing of a smoky cloud
Thirstily, earth drinks, suckles greedily
Ferocious snakes of lightning, thundering loud
A day changed so ominously; violently!

Rivers burp and break their banks
They even rival the cursed sea!
Drenched in black with warships and tanks
This heart has lost it's only quay …

In all this confused fuss and fear
So few; so few hearts conquer
More ripped by the callous tear!
How futile is loves, allure ….

So dull is this day…
Rain, tears, blood and bone soaked soil.
Tomorrow flowers will have their a say
Today, they float in disarray, seeding in turmoil!

LOVE IS BUT A BUTTERFLY

A loneliness so soothing, sinking then floating……………………

A faint flutter touches my starkly, cold and plain skin!

A ferocious fire torches my curiously, coy heart

A soft caressing brushes my startled hand

A fiery rush flushes my ashen cheeks

A weaving, cascading of colour

Intertwined, by a body of delicate
love, so infatuating. Striking wings painted! §…. passion, caressing senses,
enticing. Soaring to flamboyant heights in unison. Slowly, softly, stoked, stirred into one. Revels in nature's
tasty, liberal, alluring, sweet luxuries §…with opulence and fun. Suckling nectar tenderly, hungrily, spreading,
flitting, flirting, nurturing beautiful butterfly, loved in fragility, so freely fleeting agility eternally!

A token of love unsought

A tender, tactile creature of love

A creation concocted from the blue sky

A fancy flight of zig-zagging, in transient bliss

A blaze of butterflies, an eternal sighing agonizing kiss!…..

A sadly drenched brevity of beauty harrowing……………………

HUNGER

A burning wretched pain
The mind goes pitifully insane
A gnawing curse grows malignant within
The abused, forlorn heart falls prey to a bin!

The violently beaten mind now racing
Putrid thoughts, once pure, now menacing
An evil workshop beckoning
Unleashes; a morbid, unthinkable thing!

A feeble, empty, love-craving heart
forlorn from the promising start…
Daggered, parched ; left for dead,
Now begging to be fed!

Too confused, abused and broken
The heart feeds off the filthy bin.
"You dare, humiliate, emasculate me, whore!
I'll break you to pieces, he hissed and swore!"

Wait till judgement day arrives
Behold all the crushed lives
His ignorant innocence, he pleads
Truth, he abuses… and astray he leads!

Now…. when a soul hungers for a love beyond
A love of light in God's arms bound
Angels cry to the universe…
" Imbue true love over this inhumane curse!"

MIRROR

Mirror … oh! … Mirror … you dreaded thing!
But for truth …, only admiring.
You cunningly know what the ego craves …
We sheepishly are your soul sold slaves!

How we look.. searching your shiny blank eyes
But all you do, is hypnotise…
For reality sake, fake beautiful immortality
Seconded by the truth of eternity!
Shattered, I am ready, pierce my heart!

It's only the start.
Deep breath…, eyes shut …, the truth stark
Shattering the dark!

"I'm shattered to a brittle,
This truth from my metal,
Still every speck of my soul,
Reveals the whole!"

The pond, river, lake
Your sins they will take
And when tranquility restores
You realize the cause …

Then at once, a mirror's blank gaze
… is placidly placed over your face.
In this truth, you need no words or lies
For plainly you reflect a wanton disguise.

THE TEAR

The words – a pebbled, watery mind
Freezes …
A simmering, smoldering heart
Ceases
A venomous potion brews…
A parched pout ; A slight bruise
A pleading, floundering, weakly beating heart
As helical hearts sever… apart!

The argumentative heart stops to implode!
A scathing assault at an intellect, on hold.
A violent crushing of glass and soul!
A diabolical disrespect of a body; mine sole!
A satanic spell upon a mind!
Souls shatter from a slash of this kind!

The verdict: search haphazardly ; within…
A pristine love now seeks a foul bin!
A universal heartbreak in a split second!
A resilient residue of God won't let you end…
A doomed, deflated heart won't stop now
For time shall thread the truth of the Tao!

UNIVERSAL SURRENDER

Let's waft into the universe
Close your eyes, breathe don't curse
The other world beckons
For unblemished hearts its takes but seconds.

To dissolve in a soft vastness
A vastness of selflessness
Unfathomable
Of which every heart is capable.

A still, humming essence of silence.
Cascading peace and penance
A glimpse of our maker.
Guarded is this code breaker

This rare and mysterious moment
Shuns fiercely minds that ferment
Then the universe bares all
… insidious people are covered in gall!

This stroll among the stars,
To limp, such a farce
Explosively exfoliating smarks
…now surrounded by sacred sparks…

And, I melt into space
A lover's chaste embrace
Nourished by the Sun
Swirl and converge; WE ARE BUT ONE!

UNIVERSE PERVADING

Each and everyone of us
comes sheathing something within.
The absolute final touch from God…
"TAKE CARE MY CHILD; BE SURE TO LISTEN"

This voice speaks clearly and quick..
From the universes - a Golden String!
Conquering a hundred billion lies
From it only angels naggingly sing!

Some snigger and mockingly laugh…
over wound by a maddened, menial mind
Yet even the demonic, Golden Strung,
in stillness, the truth they find!

Some resonate, placidly knowing
these invisible quantum vibrations..
and resounding universes…,
in holy joyful celebrations!

An eagerly awaiting universe
Pulsates in motherly, patient anxiety
For when that single, sincere, ionic thought…
is succinctly translated to sublime tranquility!

A UNIVERSE DROPPED

Billions of lives in a speck, a drop.
Then you get it, in awe you STOP!
The naked eye, unashamedly ignorant
of this blessed universes' God-sent!

Play God, it's easy, it's grand
Now your ego, your folly surely is fanned
Lights, Lens, Actions; Beguiled you're glued.
They live, eat, play; There's bad and good.

The useful, you will abuse
The bad, the bad will use
Just let them be, for after some tested time
Starve them, putrid," THEY'LL DIE!" you mime!

When ego swollen hands eventually spill
This unleashed monster, goes for the kill!
The invisible blow lethal more than any gun
No! you Can't!…. would God run???

Festering fast…, dash, decipher!!!
Decree of integrity; concurrently concur!
Now kill the bad, don't just stare!
Abnormally abominable, how did you dare???
You claim power over evil, show potential…
Yet it thrives, OH GOD! IT'S NOW EXPONENTIAL!
With your microscope, yes, you can KILL…
With clenched fists, people lay STILL!

This scientific freak, "I'm God!" he said.
Now kneeling over, bowed head and dead
Gripped white in death, he prayed a first!
What of us, whom you've doomed and cursed!?

HAPPINESS

I choose happiness.
Stopped chasing my shadow
With darkness behind; in circles I'm bound…
With darkness ahead; I crush to the ground!

This happiness I chose
Fleeting highs, ebbing lows

And if it were free
We'd summerly dance.
Invisible monsters kind and bad
Malign the mind; benignly clad!

Choose happiness I sigh
Simply live, happily die …

Enter with ears
Tied to heart's golden string
Practise, stay patient, take that fall
Hoods off; the universe heeds your call!

When happiness happens aglow
Skyward we soar, look not below

Then the truth be told
Of the secret nectar we sense
Abundantly it wafts, drenching the air
Capture it swift; drink with care!

Happiness torches the heart of a cell
Your core oozes volcanically, you'll tell

Mum died yesterday …   Happily you'll say…Her pain and sorrows
Now taken away Happiness she reaps is what you pray.

If only this happiness would happily stay.
Like some despicable mind, it decides to stray
I grovel, I groan, clawing, I reach out to him
Says I'm too clingy…. Throws me out on a limb!

SECRETIVE SEA

As I merrily walked along the beach
The sea sighed shorely, whispering,
Are you here to love, learn or teach?
Nudging, Nagging, Longing, Lingering!

Millions of billions of crystals of sand
coarsely caressing; crusting my feet
As I tried to listen and understand,
Fate, the horizon I must meet!

Am I?; Am I not?; You are…; NO! You're NOT!
Waves of trepidation seek deep; gently severe
Should I change, renounce; accept my LOT…?
Or these quaint marvels of my God revere?

You've created confusion my dearest God!
At times a mother, a delightfully delinquent child
…. this life is a four-edged sword!
I live this life the way You've styled!

Maybe in the flowing of energy
Sublimely created, never destroyed,
lies an eternal secret of synergy
of this higher presence, my heart's void

I let this throbbing force, wet my lithe feet
…. Flow a sure, pure, divine course
where body, mind and soul meet,
To ignite some sacred source.

With every said sacred step I renew!
Nothingness of space seeps soft through me
 Each cells tiny brain, it scans through
Soon, swiftly with my soul I start to see!!!

MAGIC MOON

So pitifully, ever-wanting; there is no other
So resplendent; a soulmate's contentment
O! I'm barren without my lover!
Yet, he watches the Earth flirt by

I glow alive, bathed in your fiery glance
The nights glow, burning a slow death!
You are mine, yet I nourish her
That sphere, my fear, my spectre

Who suffers most – the World of course!
You dared tread by to eclipse my love

"NOW, SUFFER THIS CURSE!"

We were meant to be oh, glorious one
I was radiant and free; Yet she scorns darkness over me

"THE ONES THAT ECLIPSE ME…

I'LL WREAK HAVOC; SPINNING THEIR GLORIOUS SEA!

DARED TO TRESPASS MY ILLUMINOUS LOVE, MY LIFE AND ME!!!"

I'LL PULL ON THEIR WATERS…. WRECKING THEIR LIVES, THEIR ECONOMY!

I'LL LAUGH IN LOUD DERISION, WHEN THEIR HEADS TURN ON EACH OTHER!

I SPIT POISON ON THEIR GROWING FOOD AND WATCH THEM BEG MERCY!

THIS POWER I WIELD, BATHE AND FEEL, FOOLS TOO CLEVER TO SEE??

CURSE, I'LL IMPLODE, THEY'LL EXPLODE, INSANE AM I, KILL ME

MY CALM NIGHTS, THEY TOOK TO REVEL IN SECRECY

BATHED BARED ABANDONED ME

Without you I die an insignificant death
With your radiance there's oneness
This thread we share of NOTHINGNESS…
Aliens and distance, MEANINGLESS…
These atoms of love piercing the VASTNESS….

VULTURES

A tormented, fragmented mind
A broken, bruised body, curled and crushed
The death of my love signed
Stopping my Heart, so maligned!

A vulture began to circle and hover
for that merciless moment of tear!
(ALAS! Even angels tearing, frightfully took Cover!)
Thus, consuming my heart, became my lover!

Then vultures clawed, ripped, shredded in mirth
Devouring hungrily this suffering sin
Battling for release from death
for reunion with mother Earth …

The cycle of life, love and fulfillment
Precariously balanced ego
Patient; Impatient; Fickle; Lament
Shun : There's something permanent

Tangled entrails stench and bitterly bloat ;
Poisoned blood dissipating thoughts
of a felled victim, the vultures gloat
He loved - BUT WHERE WAS MY MOAT?

Back to the frenzied, fiasco feeding
A soul surviving carcass, walking talking
Words and gait, of soulless bleeding
Vultures filthily cleaned up ; revelingly revealing!

GOD'S HANDS

Finally after all I've studied
There's a graceful, powerful, peaceful
sensation that stirs; pulsates deep
A connection through my heart I keep.

It was but yesterday I knew not
Of this golden thread of love unsaid
Touched by a caress of blissfulness,
… A long forgotten mother's carefulness.
Today there's something I almost feel

A magic carpet; a puppet string…
And then, when I so myself resign,
Nature's embrace makes everything mine!

Look with eyes closed in search
Then, with every rising sun falling you'll see
That distinct cradle of His outstretched Palm..
In anticipation and hope of a gifted Psalm.

And when you take that really big fall
And feel you've slipped right through His
Fingers,
in one of His millions of billions of Hands
your bruised soul, soulfully lands!

Dazed and baffled, you regain your step
Your glassy emotions shattered and spilled
nothing you feel, not your soul…
So He draws in deeply, now you're whole.
As aimlessly I try to self-destruct my VIRTUOUSNESS..
" YOU HOLD MY SWIRL, THIS ECLIPSED LOVE IN PURE SELFISHNESS!"

HIS AWARD

In this robotic body and
well-wired brain,
Pumps the heart of flesh and light
This creation, Insane!

"I'VE OVERDOSED ON MY ESSENCE,
SURELY, SHE'LL SURPASS ME IF NOT FOR SINS"
Flow for blow, she rises each time ....!
In Time we shall see her restrains…

Her man, her blood attacked her,
dented, scratched, blue and few wires out!
But the Golden Thread's still there!
"TOUCH HER BLOOD AND YOU DROWN IN THE MOAT!"

Tears in His Eyes

" EVEN I HAVE NOT THAT COMPASSION! "
Smiling in awe, He takes her hand….
Seats her next to Himself, this companion!
Now meek and satiated…

She takes it in, this Queen
At home in His ethereal world.
Now, only with Him she'll be seen!
Her worldly one despises her as fiend

How she ravaged his weak worldly heart!
… when that law of consequence was induced!
A smash that shook him smart
shredding his world apart!

MUSTANG

Biting cold wind; violent rain
Swirled her regal white silken mane
Around her slender strong royal neck
Fiery eyes he stood, as a raw speck!
… beauty so rare she stood almost vain!
Mesmerizing was this magnificent Mustang
But in the wind, something eerily unholy sang!
Graciously wild, free-spirited, so spiritual
admiration that would conquer was eventual!
…a heartfelt pang…
Men rounded up, "… snared without injury
she must be whole, intelligence over fury!
succumbing willfully, capture the foal
living in her mind, body and soul!"
Please, God's jury!

Spirited beauty, purity and grace …
exhilarating his heart, this whimsical chase.
A meaningless want, unquenchable reign
Blinded were all, by this cursed love feign
… an unholy mace!

Yet, it did and she was snared…!
He rejoiced, "Treasured, never impaired!"
Days grew dark, a swollen heart owned
In silence and despair loneliness groaned.
Scared, uncared!

The strain insidiously, started to show
in a new fenced world, she just began to know
A realm of opulent starvation, degradation
sinister systemic suffocation.
Heavens aglow!

A writhing spirit, slowly, sickly suffered
Yet her strength, of a thousand men, offered.
Angels appalled, then came that fateful day
Bloodied and battered his heart, equally lay
Conquered!

Though beauty burnt deathly in eyes, hallow
Conquest over love proves eternally shallow.
Love is not love when won by a whim.
Love is but love, the heart's eternal hymn.
Heed the winds bellow!

VOICES

I listened to the voice inside my head,
analysing everything that it said.
My constant companion in love and crime,
Telling me everything would heal in time-
That I would be a fool to defy…
Advice of a sinister, yet good lie!
Flying into a rage I would be praised…
Having broken a heart I would stand amazed
What exactly did this booming voice create?
Whose appetite…, broken hearts satiate!
Fight with all your might! You're Right, You're Right, so perfectly Right!

Then I hear a little voice in my heart
Not manipulative, yet it stood apart!
A still, soothing silence, it's essence eternal
Like a drop of God, something maternal
and if I didn't listen well and good
My parched heart murmured, I should.
For when sporadically, I tuned in…
I was enveloped in light away from sin!
We swim in silt of love and hate.
In this microcosm of a centered universe, wait!
Spiritualize, you realize, you realize you are REALIZED!

AFTERMATH

Silence, it's over
Shocked into peace
Carnage, festering emotions at my feet
Disdain cloaked in love …

Violated Heart throttled
Caressing hand; clenched, punches
Worshipped footsteps
Righteously kicking
Bodies relentless in the name of love…

Who pulled the trigger
Bloodied, blur to see
When hearts had merged
Like a mirage at sea
So dry, so dark, so die!

An explosive SILENCE….
Now we free
Vortex my soul
My return …. I'm whole
The release, violent streaming violet
A soft swaying feather
Nothingness

Nothingness.

Nothingness…

FOR LOVE OF THE WORLD

The inner sanctum relented…
Rage, passion, love,… Dissipated
Pure, innocent love pound,
Gregariously, gnashed and ground.

The seed of love, a blossoming soul
Tried desperately to embrace him whole.
Acts of love so free, euthanized, or so it be,
blinded and deaf, he just couldn't see!!!

He needed them, they fulfilled a need.
Respect, care, humanitarian indeed
Cheerful, trusting, compassionate
Teamed, they toiled in companionship…

So love in despair scavenged for love and caring
But disgusted all by a futile, despicable, filthy veering!
So pained, drained and insane, ..
that love, love did feign

The avalanche of despair was triggered
by base wisdom that had figured
balancing uncaring abuse with lusty disarray
…. he constantly drove love astray!

TRANSITION: SOLE JOURNEY

Wide-eyed, unblemished, love-divine
cradled by love undefined
celestial laughter, jubilant crawl
precocious, pending fall.
Heartening awe
Reassured, coaxed some more
Freedoms walked
Parentally stalked…

Wings of wisdom sprout
In worldly dreams caught
Dwellings decked palatially
Car furious, luxurious
Fisted, designed, fitted
Status Exclusive
Happiness elusive

Something gives, forgives
Ignites within, a spark lives
The journey timeless
Souls restless …

Now a sickly sweet mango
Wait…, the fall; the seed will sow!
Painfully, faithfully, fruitfully to plan
This cyclic prison, born as man.
Aged in pain, so curing
Look at your tree, soaring
Everything whirling into one
Look, Look to the sun!
A journey so solely endless
Ending in misery when careless

                                        If conceived

            …would you have perceived?

JOCK

He talks to my heart with huge, innocent eyes
No words from him, so he tells no lies
Brindle and angelic white, hand-painted Perfection
One word from me, he bounds into
Action

I gather him close, I listen to his heart
I pray, I miss God's love when we're apart
Forgives my sins, lavishes me with love,
respect and trust
He is redemption, love not lust.

A torrent of wildly dancing leaps of love…
selfless, no boundaries
unbridled love, my soul it frees….

Just us two, populate his world,
Tears of thanks for this love, I see curled.

Deep in innocent dreams he deliriously jerks…
Snarling, scratching, slurping … Best of all he
smirks!

Fighting, Barking, Yelping … Protecting me Still
I take a deep breath, I laugh, of this love,
I take my fill

My hand touches his warm, dry nose.
A weak wag of gratitude, then his eyes close.

Content, blood-shot eyes roll in and out of ; Reality
I hug my love, my haven, from harsh Eventuality

Wide-awake, he puts his once iron paw on what's his to own
His ball, squeaky toy, blanky, his bone!

A heart-stopping sound, a growl, a glance… I'm first on his mind…
My spouse; a stark disjoint I find!

Dear God cradle him, this love of Yours ….
So Free!
If I've earned any good from You, Please
Let Jock take from me.

Literally poles apart
Spirit and soul wrenched from the heart
The lights go out
What are you about?

> This euphoric dilemma
> Then the devil's murmur
> The lulls of life appease me
> I take a breath, I see

God speaks to me in green
Beauty and life expressingly, keen
Intensely I take in this blade of grass
The poles draw closer; if only a farce

> So still, so quiet the basis of life
> My other side cursedly cuts like a knife
> If only I could be centred and quiet
> And not down, upon this dreary plight…!

With this blade of grass I hold God's hand
It's drawing closer for me to take a stand
Weakened by disappointment, a mere agitation
Reels me into a demonic dimension…

> Got to get there and pull myself together
> A sacred glue I pray for, my dear Father
> I look at the desolate destruction
> I feel cursed, lonely; no solution

> My loved ones whom I ruthlessly stab
> Their love, patience and compassion;
> MY ONLY REHAB!

UNIVERSAL LOVE

A universe of colour-filled black
Shimmering stars, intense glowing suns
The benevolent eye of our God
A nebula watches detachedly,
Nothingness expanding exponentially!

A galaxy of force-filled yellow
Swirled in peerless precision
A far-flung magnified atom
Pulsating magnificently,
Silent, quiet, steered majestically

A planet of water-filled green
Cocooned in the breath of life
From the purse of our Lord
A myriad life forms burst vibrantly
Everything's resonating harmoniously

A soul of pure light-filled white
Shrouded by ignorance
A subtle clue of our God!
Ten thousand hearts discover daily
Something living deep within, eternally!

OH MY GOD!

His Eyes, they reflect the universe
To love Him: a flippant, foregone curse
His Hair a mysterious black cascade
But then a blinding, blessed destiny played!

This elusive Lover, a guiding force
.... turning brutal and coarse.
Beautiful, comforting and sensually divine
Flinging my love to pills and wine!

I sincerely prayed and openly begged
... with loving eyes, my name He pegged
for Him to be my one and only
... next to arduous, metal, truth, and solely

He sent forth lovers and pitiful pleasure
He tossed a rope - would I measure?
My path strewn in folly soaked ego
I tried, stumbled; felled - should I let go?

My grip, sawing fire, volcanizing, agonizing
Succumbing to a love so spiritualizing
Body debased, mind mazed, soul derailed.
Rope shredded flesh, in blood it trailed

" Now, if in this first test you own your own "
... HE said softly, in a pensive tone,
" and when I feel your love to be true...
... surely, I shall fall in love with you too! "

CAN GOD BE THERE?

Dear God, each time I think I've got it…
You move a piece to check.
Too splendidly ignorant to quit it…
Spiritually indisposed ; I fling "Oh! heck!"

There's a chip intrinsically, me!
The signal's so strong, then so weak…
Glancing in trepidation, I inwardly see
Clearly why I should be meek.

For this ignored connection in us…
It's so inconspicuously complete
Still, remain still amidst the fuss
This is life's feat.., Defeat!

My hands are full, my heart, so tired…
Body's broken, mind's blown apart!
You've dealt; I've played; I've tried
Treading lightly, I'll closet, this reckless heart!

Sobered, I truly can't remember
This…, did I actually seek?
"Rumination", next I'll, choose to bear!
 Within my mind… an oceanic forest creek!!!

But I'm here now,… Love's silly sorrow
"I tell You God, sincerely, loud and clear,
if not today, then surely tomorrow…
this heart, You'll leave, like a drop of tear!"

This Golden drop You so bless
You know it all, I feel so bare ….
My mind in squalor such a mess
Instill essence, Please show You there….!

TIRED HEART

They've all gone
For a few hours.
Of me born
Yet higher powers

Lavish, peaceful tranquility
Now, I don't feel guilty

Love them tenaciously!
Love him, desperately?

These numb moments start…
         What do they say?
A balm to a tired heart
A mother's soul driven away…

My children, my breath
My love, I fret …

Why this lightness
an hour… not more?
Then I'm aimless
I've no core!!!

God-charged moments, fleeted
Heart-reboot successfully completed!!!

EMBRACE YOURSELF

Take a deep breath, NO; Deeper…
A surfeit of Nothingness
None more Sweeter!

Gaze distantly, NO; Farther …
That fathomless-etched Skyline…
It's the hand of your Father!

Ear to ground now listen, NO; Closer…
The soothing, seething silence
Mother earth's heart in rhythmic pulsar!

Chew on this blade of grass, NO; Savour…
Bursting, burning, spreading, potent green
A Dynamic, unknown spiritual flavour!

Feel the breezed sunshine, NO; Stronger…
This celestial caress, lulling limitlessness
This embrace… eternally longer!

Now that you are aware, NO; Alive…
Bathe, frolic in the depths of Timelessness
This mundane existence you'll survive!

Love from the heart, NO; Soully…
This constellation… a singular Congregation
Tap into your source, live wholly!

BLINDING LOVE

Her eyes speak heavenly bliss
Her touch hellish passion
Her lips soft and curiously they kiss
Unrequited soul stirring... caution!

Those mundane eyes in innocence shine
Burn blank pointed, tormenting a fickle mind
Coyly, callously they say, "You're mine..."
And toy with you like some precious find!

Love and passion intertwined in a deathly grip
parasitically, nibble the heart and stab the soul
materially you, they strip...
Ruthlessly you've turned in a ghoul!

Lust masquerading as love and passion
Love is not of this world, we're strung!
To grasp this..., Life's elusive lesson
Reigning Love's golden strings, He is but One!

A purest, warm, serene light
A maze secretly, sacredly dungeoned
Locked in the chest; you ignite
For your heart to be bludgeoned!

GOD BLINKED

White Stars and the moon Caress
the contours of a sleepy Earth.
Hearts were tied to so impress
When love fell and then souls took birth …

Hearts and souls chasmed apart
Short-lived; and eternally true
Forlorn love ruptures the heart
Soul sapping mundane Love... carnally grew!

Time handed down the sentence.
These two were, however, acquitted.
Love, loved only in defence
Soul free, the sky with diamonds was littered!

God blinked that fateful moment
during this soul-heart mauling match…
When such and such souls are sent
Will God make that prayed, brilliant catch?

THE CITY LIGHTS

Faceted, coloured congregation
By day a soulful, spirited nation
Shimmering minds, bodies, souls and spirit
By night restless minds, the devious culprit

I look from my pedestal
This man-mountain swallows the sun; and still
I look beyond the blocks of building blocks
Bustlingly entering my chest; it mocks

The taxis like bulimic bugs, noisily, they chirp
sensing darkness, slowly their time will usurp
People scurry and ant-like they surge
As mountain and sky in blackness merge!

When the cool, crisp, soft cotton sheets
cushion and caress my smile-worn cheeks
An invisible monster of blatant deceits.
Cloaked in black; the wayward it seeks.

Throat-throttling laughter, demonic taunts
A marauding motorbike massacre ; haunts
Stabs at my windows, claws at the walls.
OH! my hollow body shudders from lewd calls.

Police sirens swirl my mind, my heart, my soul
… suffocated, smothered, by the black ghoul!
Revellers, curse, soiling the night atrociously
Dismembered I fight at this vortex, viciously!

As I pray, I cling to God
give me light, glorious light my… LORD
Grappling, I choke; seeing savagery by satan!
But the long dark night is stealthy and latent.

My mind tormented, tossed, in tatters
My heart exploded, and bloodily scatters
Body drained pale; black night tattoos my eyes
My soul's afloat and in my Lord's hands lies.

Then alas, God-sent light in praise.
Carelessly throwing her flamboyant rays
The city slowly regains consciousness
Signaling a vicious cycle, I guess.

WHAT IF I ALREADY WANT YOU, LORD?

Forward …, Backward …,
Skyward …, Outward …,
Finally …… Inward!
The search goes Onward …

OH, Dear One … Please reveal
The reason: Layers… and layers peel ….
Do You revel at this vessel's scathing sea?
Whatever Your holy reason be?
Dear God, this is insanity …
None so blind as those who will not see.
Soul Tattered; Heart Torn, I truly only want THEE…
I've bruised my body…
Realised its nothing to me…
I've mangled my mind …
Sometimes, even to the devil it's signed!!!
I've hacked my heart…
Some, solace it did impart!!!
But my soul… my soul….

Fervently I clawed for my wayward soul
Bloodied hands drenched; dripping so foul
When I knifed into my beating, bleating chest!
Couldn't find my soul …. should have guessed!

CONCEIVABLE INTIMACY

There's a certain friendship
…where unuttered hintings flit
…a mysteriously malignant sort
… leaves you snared and caught…
… Between humans, being fraught

There's certainly warmth and comfort
Straining… awkwardly in a shot.
Streaming current.
A wicked torrent.
boisterous infatuation apparent.

There's certainly passion…
Doubting, disengaging emotion
of a flammable gnawing kind,
lavishly, consumed body, signed
Deliriously, desirously, satanly, insaned!!!

There's a certain eventual end
A soul-boiling event, God will send
A chasmed spirit; curtly restored
… Intimacy entwined with the Lord
Murky-watered lotus, the golden chord!